MY LITTLE
Book of Prayers

ILLUSTRATED BY
KATHY ALLERT

A Golden Book • New York
Western Publishing Company, Inc.
Racine, Wisconsin 53404

ACKNOWLEDGMENTS

"Thank you, God, for this new day," from *The Infant Teacher's Prayer Book*, edited by D. M. Prescott, reprinted by permission of Blandford Press. "A great gray elephant," © 1942, reprinted by permission of the National Society to Prevent Blindness. "Dear God, I gratefully bow my head," by Dixie Willson, reprinted by permission of Dana W. Briggs. "Father, thank You for the night," by Dale Evans Rogers, reprinted by permission of Dale Evans Rogers.

Now before I run to play,
  Let me not forget to pray
To God who kept me
    through the night
And waked me with the
    morning light.

Thank you, God, for this new day,
And for the time to work and play.
Please be with me all day long,
In every story, game, and song.
May all the happy things we do
Make you, our Father, happy too.

To do to others as I would
  That they should do to me,
Will make me gentle, kind, and good,
  As children ought to be.

A great gray elephant,
A little yellow bee,
A tiny purple violet,
A tall green tree,
A red and white sailboat
On a blue sea—
All these things
You gave to me,
When you made
My eyes to see—
    Thank you, God!

Where is God?
In the sun, the moon, the sky,
On the mountains, wild and high,
In the thunder, in the rain,
In the vale, the wood, the plain,
In the little birds that sing,
God is seen in everything.

Praise and gratitude to you, Holy Father,
Who created the skies and heaven first
And after that created the big wet sea
And the heaps of fish in it swimming closely.
—ANCIENT IRISH HYMN

All things bright and beautiful,
All creatures great and small,
All things wise and wonderful,
The Lord God made them all.

—C. F. ALEXANDER

Dear Father, hear and bless
Thy beasts and singing birds:
And guard with tenderness
Small things that have no words.

Loving Friend, oh hear our prayer,
Take into Thy tender care,
All the leaves and flowers that sleep
In their white bed covered deep.
Shelter from the wintry storm
All the snow birds: keep them warm.

—SARA E. WILTSE

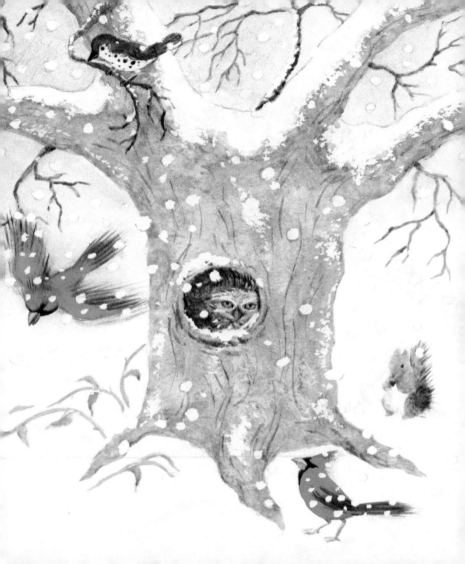

The wee bird has its nest,
  Safe in the tree so tall;
For birdlings' nests, for children's homes,
I thank the Lord for all.

Dear God, I gratefully bow my head
To thank You for this daily bread;
And may there be a goodly share
On every table everywhere. Amen.

—DIXIE WILLSON

Thank You for the world so sweet;
Thank You for the food we eat;
Thank You for the birds that sing;
Thank You, God, for everything!

—E. RUTTER LEATHAM

Father, thank You for the night,
Thank You for the day,
For the chance to do some work
And for the chance to play.

Thank You for my family,
Father, Mother, too,
And for all my playmates,
But most of all for You.

—DALE EVANS ROGERS

God watches o'er us all the day,
At home, at school, and at our play;
And when the sun has left the skies,
He watches with a million eyes.

—GABRIEL SETOUN

I see the moon,
And the moon sees me;
God bless the moon,
And God bless me.

Now I lay me down to sleep,
I pray Thee, Lord, thy child to keep;
Thy love go with me all the night,
And wake me with the morning light.